ACCESSORIES
OPTIONS

LEISURE ARTS, INC.
Little Rock, Arkansas

ISBN 1-57486-587-0

ACCESSORIES
OPTIONS

Have you ever been tempted to use an altogether different yarn than the one recommended by your knitting pattern?

To help you envision the results you would get from a second yarn choice, Leisure Arts' **exciting** new **Options** books show you not only the original designer creation, but a second design in an entirely **different** brand and color of yarn.

The delightful results in *Options: Accessories* are a collection of **ten stylish designs** in **two** yarn variations by Margie Morse Pulley. Whatever your skill level, our thorough instructions will have you finishing your scarf, stole, shawl, or shrug with ease.

You'll have the look that's perfect for you!

Margie Morse Pulley

Margie Morse Pulley is a business owner, a wife, and a mother of three. She is also a witness to the connections between knitting, friendship, and miracles.

In 1999, Margie's daughter, then just six years old, became ill with an autoimmune disease that affected her eyes. Seemingly endless weeks of waiting began for Margie. She spent hours in doctor's offices and hospitals while her daughter received treatment. Through it all, knitting helped. "My mother sat with me and taught me the stitches," Margie says. "We called it 'medical knitting.'"

Just when life seemed to settle into a more normal routine, Margie was stunned to learn that she also suffers from an autoimmune disease. And once again, knitting was there for her.

"My blood work was done in the same facility where oncology patients are treated. To while away the time, I just kept thinking that when I felt better, I was going to do something I really loved. I decided I wanted to open a knitting shop. I told my husband what I had in mind. His support was immediate and has been unfailing ever since.

"So I prayed, 'Lord, is this what You want me to do?' And my answer came in the form of doors opening up to me. Only they didn't just open in the normal fashion — they *flew* open.

"The first thing I did was visit a friend who works at a local bank. I told him what I was thinking and I asked him if I could have a small business loan. To my surprise, he simply said, 'okay.'

"The next step was finding a location. There was one in particular that I really wanted for my shop. I knew in my heart it was the right place, the perfect place for a yarn shop. And the day I went by to check on it was the very same day the owner placed a For Rent sign in the window.

"We opened Bella Lana Knitting in less than three months. That was eighteen months ago."

Smooth oak shelves line the walls of the new shop. Each compartment offers an abundance of fine yarn. The tempting skeins have become a familiar indulgence for many of Margie's regular customers. The wealth of color and texture attracts passersby who are delighted to learn that they, too, can knit.

In the center of the store are a large table and a generous number of chairs. This is where Margie's customers gather for classes and the once-a-month Ladies' Night Out. And the table is often occupied by customers who just drop by to visit.

"The most unusual friendships get started when knitting is involved," says Margie. "My nineteen-year-old shop assistant has become a bosom buddy to a regular customer who is in her early sixties. And right now," Margie indicates three ladies currently at the table, "the wife of a missionary to Nigeria, a former Madison Avenue executive, and my assistant are all knitting and whooping it up over there." As if on cue, there is a burst of laughter and loud conversation.

The shop does seem to be an answered prayer for Margie, who continues to knit for relaxation as well as for physical therapy. There is a metal plate in her hand, a result of her illness. "Knitting is the perfect exercise for my hand," she says. "It keeps it from hurting."

Margie also found herself knitting out of necessity. "When we opened the shop, it seemed there were very few knitting patterns for beginners. So I started designing easy scarves and worked my way up. Now that ponchos are popular again, I've designed several in simple patterns.

"...while knitting enables you to create a great garment, it can also help you build some amazing friendships."

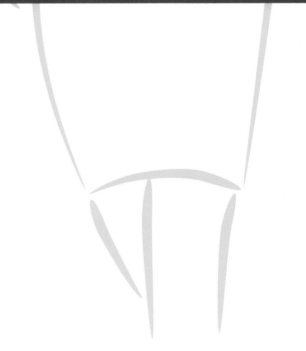

"I think people enjoy the results of knitting because it's fun to see someone's jaw drop when they realize you made the poncho, scarf, or sweater you're wearing. And it's even better to see someone you love wearing something you made for them.

"Knitting really is the new yoga, the new left brain/right brain exercise. And while knitting enables you to create a great garment, it can also help you build some amazing friendships."

Judging by the enthusiastic outbursts at the shop's worktable, Margie's customers couldn't agree more.

CONTENTS

A BIT BOHEMIAN **OPTION 1**

Softness that embraces your shoulders or hangs gracefully from your hips — this **versatile** shawl/belt accessory is fashioned from brown/black short eyelash yarn to create a **richness** you can see and feel.

OPTION ②

Don't be shy! Add **pizzazz** to your day with this **colorful** version of our self-fringing shawl/belt. Leave subtlety to someone else — this is your day to **shine**!

Option 1

Crystal Palace Yarns® Shag
Bulky Weight Short Eyelash Yarn
[1³/₄ ounces, 57 yards (50 grams, 52 meters)
per skein]: #7201 (Brown/Black) - 3 skeins

Straight knitting needles, size 17 (12.75 mm) **or**
size needed for gauge

GAUGE: In Stockinette Stitch, 10 sts = 4" (10 cm)

A BIT BOHEMIAN ◖▮▯▭ EASY

Option 2

Bernat® Boa
Bulky Weight Short Eyelash Yarn
[1³/₄ ounces, 71 yards (50 grams, 65 meters)
per skein]: #81303 Doo Doo Bird - 2 skeins

Straight knitting needles, size 17 (12.75 mm) **or**
size needed for gauge

GAUGE: In Stockinette Stitch, 10 sts = 4" (10 cm)

Shawl/Belt

Cast on 5 sts.

Row 1: Purl across.

Row 2 (Right side – Increase row)**:** K3, increase by knitting into the front and back loop of the next st *(Figs. 2a & b, page 47)*, K1: 6 sts.

Row 3: Purl across.

Row 4 (Increase row)**:** K3, increase, knit across: 7 sts.

Rows 5-46: Repeat Rows 3 and 4, 21 times: 28 sts.

Row 47: Purl across.

Row 48 (Decrease row)**:** K3, K2 tog *(Fig. 5, page 48)*, knit across: 27 sts.

Rows 49-93: Repeat Rows 47 and 48, 22 times; then repeat Row 47 once **more**: 5 sts.

Row 94: Knit across; pass the second st on right needle over the first st, cut yarn and pull end through loop: 3 sts.

FRINGE

Slowly unravel the 3 edge sts on every row, one row at a time, tying an overhand knot at base of each loop, close to piece.

GO FOR GLAMOUR

OPTION 1

For **special** occasions, you may want a little something extra to go with your favorite attire. The **sparkling** metallic threads of this yarn are enhanced by a **gleaming** brooch. The fashion jewelry keeps the stole snug around your shoulders.

When "posh" is the look you want, this little stole of **plush** yarn delivers the luxury! And it's every bit as **easy** to knit as it is elegant to wear. Nestle the brooch clasp near your shoulder for a touch of **drama**.

2

OPTION

Option 1

Lion Brand® Festive Fur
Bulky Weight Yarn

  [1³/₄ ounces, 55 yards (50 grams, 50 meters)
  per skein]: #153 Black - 2{3} skeins

Straight knitting needles, size 13 (9 mm) **or**
  size needed for gauge
Large brooch

GAUGE: In Stockinette Stitch, 14 sts = 4" (10 cm)

GO FOR GLAMOUR

◖■□□ EASY

Option 2

Bernat® Disco
Bulky Weight Yarn

  [1³/₄ ounces, 52 yards (50 grams, 47 meters)
  per skein]: #68013 Mr. Brown - 2{3} skeins

Straight knitting needles, size 13 (9 mm) **or**
  size needed for gauge
Large brooch

GAUGE: In Stockinette Stitch, 14 sts = 4" (10 cm)

Size	Finished Length	
Small	38"	(96.5 cm)
Large	42"	(106.5 cm)

Note: Instructions are written for size Small with size Large in braces { }. Instructions will be easier to read if you circle all the numbers pertaining to your size. If only one number is given, it applies to all sizes.

Stole

Cast on 4 sts.

Row 1 (Right side – Increase row): Increase by knitting into the front and back loop of the first st *(Figs. 2a & b, page 47)*, knit across: 5 sts.

*Note: Loop a short piece of yarn around any stitch to mark Row 1 as **right** side.*

Row 2: Purl across.

Rows 3-40{48}: Repeat Rows 1 and 2, 19{23} times: 24{28} sts.

Work even in Stockinette Stitch (knit one row, purl one row) until Stole measures approximately 30{34}"/76{86.5} cm from cast on edge, ending by working a **purl** row.

Next Row (Decrease row): SSK *(Figs. 6a-c, page 48)*, knit across: 23{27} sts.

Next Row: Purl across.

Repeat last 2 rows, 19{23} times: 4 sts.

Bind off remaining 4 sts in knit.

Use brooch to pin ends of Stole together for closure, positioning Stole with shaping at top edge.

OPTION

1

Be careful! This **sweet** little stole may steal your heart. The ribbon-tied wrap has **metallic** fibers that catch the light as you move. Best of all, it's a tiny **treasure** that you can finish in a twinkling.

If metallic fibers don't catch your eye, how about creating your stole with a **kaleidoscopic** blend of yarns? This slender confection is a little slice of knitted **joy**.

OPTION

2

Crystal Palace Yarns® Splash
Bulky Weight Short Eyelash Yarn
  [3¹/₂ ounces, 85 yards (100 grams, 77.5 meters)
  per skein]: #202 Black - 2 skeins

Trendsetter Yarns® Eyelash
Bulky Weight Long Eyelash Yarn
  [³/₄ ounces, 73 yards (20 grams, 67 meters)
  per skein]: #5 Black - 3 skeins

Trendsetter Yarns® Emmy
Bulky Weight Ribbon Yarn
  [1³/₄ ounces, 66 yards (50 grams, 60.5 meters)
  per ball]: #4 Red - 3 balls

Straight knitting needles, size 13 (9 mm) **or** size needed for gauge
2" (5 cm) wide Ribbon - 1¹/₂ yards (1.37 meters)
Sewing needle and thread

GAUGE: Holding one strand of each yarn together,
in Stockinette Stitch, 9 sts = 4" (10 cm)

GLEAM & GLOW ◀■■□□ **EASY**

Bernat® Boa
Bulky Weight Short Eyelash Yarn
  [1³/₄ ounces, 71 yards (50 grams, 65 meters)
  per skein]: #81104 Mocking Bird - 2 skeins

Moda Dea® Prima
Bulky Weight Long Eyelash Yarn
  [1³/₄ ounces, 72 yards (50 grams, 66 meters)
  per skein]: #3527 Turquoise - 2 skeins

Lion Brand® Trellis
Bulky Weight Ribbon Yarn
  [1³/₄ ounces, 115 yards (50 grams, 105 meters)
  per ball]: #305 Stained Glass - 1 ball

Straight knitting needles, size 13 (9 mm) **or** size needed for gauge
2" (5 cm) wide Ribbon - 1¹/₂ yards (1.37 meters)
Sewing needle and thread

GAUGE: Holding one strand of each yarn together,
in Stockinette Stitch, 9 sts = 4" (10 cm)

Finished Size: 10¹/₂" wide x 38" long
(26.5 cm x 96.5 cm)

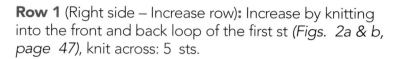

Stole

Holding one strand of each yarn together, cast on 4 sts.

Row 1 (Right side – Increase row)**:** Increase by knitting into the front and back loop of the first st (*Figs. 2a & b, page 47*), knit across: 5 sts.

Row 2: Purl across.

Rows 3-40: Repeat Rows 1 and 2, 19 times: 24 sts.

Work even in Stockinette Stitch (knit one row, purl one row) until Stole measures approximately 24" (61 cm) from cast on edge, ending by working a **purl** row.

Next Row (Decrease row)**:** SSK (*Figs. 6a-c, page 48*), knit across: 23 sts.

Next Row: Purl across.

Repeat last 2 rows, 19 times: 4 sts.

Bind off remaining 4 sts in knit.

Sew 27" (68.5 cm) length of ribbon to each end for ties.

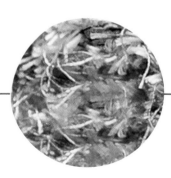

OPTION

1 A & B

Discover the many **moods** of the Long on Style scarf! Its simple pattern works up quickly and looks **fashion-savvy** in one solid hue (Option 1A). Just for fun, add a few stripes of a **funky** novelty yarn (Option 1B).

The same scarf takes a **romantic** turn in terra-cotta chenille with variegated sections (Option 2B). Or it goes **casual** in a flurry of vibrant stripes (Option 2A). Which of these **slender** scarves calls to you?

2 A & B

OPTION

Option 1A

Rowan International® Big Wool
Super Bulky Weight Yarn
[3¹/₂ ounces, 87 yards (100 grams, 80 meters)
per skein]: #024 Cassis - 2 skeins

Straight knitting needles, size 15 (10 mm) **or**
size needed for gauge

GAUGE: In Stockinette Stitch, 15 sts = 7" (17.75 cm)

LONG ON STYLE ●□□□ BEGINNER

Option 2A

Lion Brand® Wool-Ease® Thick & Quick®
Super Bulky Weight Yarn
[6 ounces, 108 yards (170 grams, 98 meters)
per skein]:
#131 Grass - 1 skein
#133 Pumpkin - 1 skein
#187 Goldenrod - 1 skein

Straight knitting needles, size 15 (10 mm) **or**
size needed for gauge

GAUGE: In Stockinette Stitch, 15 sts = 7" (17.75 cm)

Scarf

Work entire Scarf with one color or add stripes as desired.

Cast on 15 sts.

Work in Stockinette Stitch (knit one row, purl one row) until Scarf measures approximately 63" (160 cm) from cast on edge.

Bind off all sts.

Option 1B

Main Yarn:

Reynolds® Blizzard
Super Bulky Weight Yarn **SUPER BULKY 6**
  [3½ ounces, 66 yards (100 grams, 60.5 meters)
  per skein]: #641 Pink - 2 skeins

Novelty Yarns:

Trendsetter Yarns® Papi
Medium/Worsted Weight Yarn **MEDIUM 4**
  [1 ounce, 71 yards (25 grams, 65 meters)
  per skein]: #21 Pink - 1 skein

Trendsetter Yarns® Aquarius
Medium/Worsted Weight Yarn **MEDIUM 4**
  [1¾ ounces, 96 yards (50 grams, 88 meters)
  per skein]: #825 Strawberry Field - 1 skein

Trendsetter Yarns® Eyelash
Bulky Weight Long Eyelash Yarn **BULKY 5**
  [¾ ounces, 73 yards (20 grams, 67 meters)
  per skein]: #31 Raspberry - 1 skein

Straight knitting needles, size 15 (10 mm) **or**
size needed for gauge

GAUGE: With Main Yarn, in Stockinette Stitch,
12 sts = 5" (12.75 cm)

LONG ON STYLE   EASY

Option 2B

Main Yarn:

Lion Brand® Chenille "Thick & Quick"® **SUPER BULKY 6**
Super Bulky Weight Yarn [100 yards (90 meters)
  per skein]: #135 Terracotta - 1 skein

Novelty Yarn:

Lion Brand® Fancy Fur
Super Bulky Weight Long Eyelash Yarn **SUPER BULKY 6**
  [1¾ ounces, 39 yards (50 grams, 35 meters)
  per skein]: #255 Jungle Print - 1 skein

Straight knitting needles, size 15 (10 mm) **or**
size needed for gauge

GAUGE: With Main Yarn, in Stockinette Stitch,
12 sts = 5" (12.75 cm)

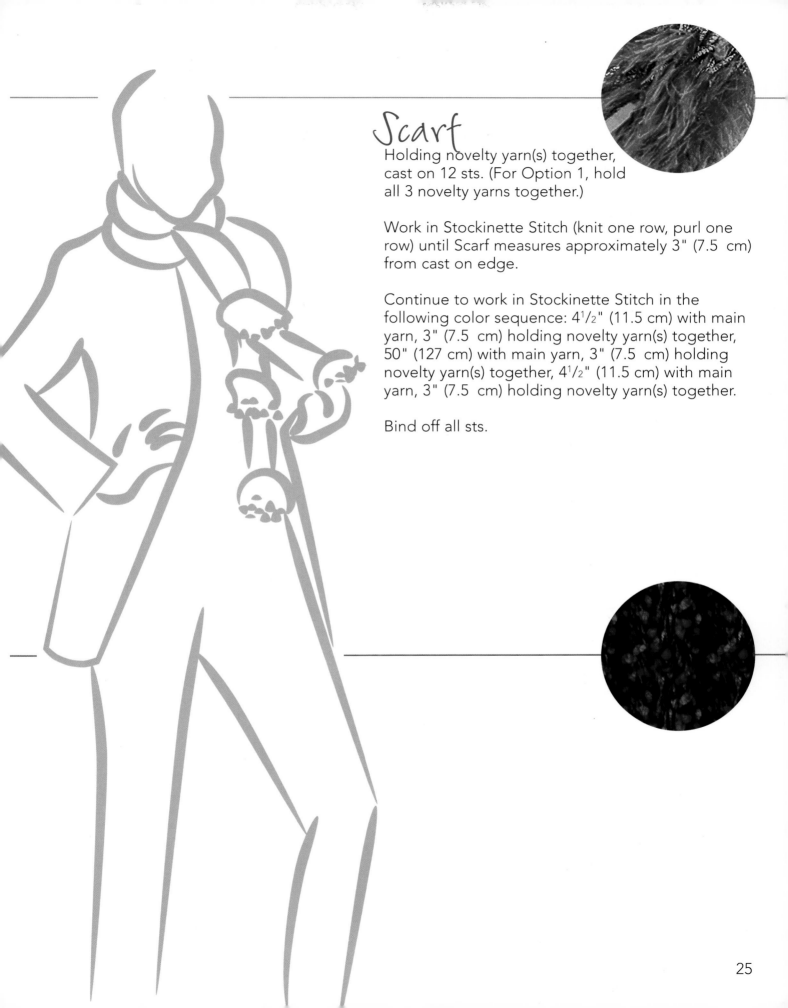

Scarf

Holding novelty yarn(s) together, cast on 12 sts. (For Option 1, hold all 3 novelty yarns together.)

Work in Stockinette Stitch (knit one row, purl one row) until Scarf measures approximately 3" (7.5 cm) from cast on edge.

Continue to work in Stockinette Stitch in the following color sequence: $4\frac{1}{2}$" (11.5 cm) with main yarn, 3" (7.5 cm) holding novelty yarn(s) together, 50" (127 cm) with main yarn, 3" (7.5 cm) holding novelty yarn(s) together, $4\frac{1}{2}$" (11.5 cm) with main yarn, 3" (7.5 cm) holding novelty yarn(s) together.

Bind off all sts.

OPTION

1

Surprise your senses with unexpected **texture**! Lime green ribbon yarn and beaded fringe give this scarf visual impact. With its upbeat, **carefree** color, you'll want to pair it with all your **weekend** wear.

Perhaps you'd prefer to have all the colors of the **rainbow** in one scarf? Choose a variegated super bulky ribbon yarn. You'll be pleased to see how well your new scarf goes with your **favorite** jackets and sweaters.

2 OPTION

Option 1

Trendsetter Yarns® Dolcino MEDIUM 4
Medium/Worsted Weight Ribbon Yarn
  [1³/₄ ounces, 99 yards (50 grams, 90 meters)
  per ball]: #109 Lime - 2 balls

Straight knitting needles, size 13 (9 mm) **or**
  size needed for gauge
Crochet hook (for fringe)
Beads - 12

GAUGE: In Garter Stitch, 15 sts = 4" (10 cm)

SHOWER OF COLOR ◖■▮▭▭◗ EASY

Option 2

Lion Brand® Incredible SUPER BULKY 6
Super Bulky Weight Ribbon Yarn
  [1³/₄ ounces, 110 yards (50 grams, 100 meters)
  per ball]: #203 City Lights - 2 balls

Straight knitting needles, size 11 (8 mm) **or**
  size needed for gauge
Crochet hook (for fringe)
Beads - 12

GAUGE: In Garter Stitch, 15 sts = 4" (10 cm)

Scarf

Cut ribbon yarn for fringe as follows and set aside: Cut a piece of cardboard 3" (7.5 cm) wide and 10" (25.5 cm) long. Wind the ribbon yarn **loosely** and **evenly** lengthwise around the cardboard 22 times, then cut across one end.

Cast on 15 sts.

Rows 1-3: Knit across.

Row 4: K1, (YO 3 times, K1) across (*Fig. 4a, page 47*): 57 sts.

Row 5: K1, (drop the 3 YO's off the needle, K1) across: 15 sts.

Rows 6 and 7: Knit across.

Repeat Rows 4-7 for pattern until Scarf measures approximately 48" (122 cm) from cast on edge **or** until desired length, ending by working Row 7.

Bind off all sts.

FRINGE

Fold one 20" (51 cm) strand of ribbon yarn in half.
With **wrong** side facing and using a crochet hook, draw the folded end up through the first stitch on cast on edge and pull the loose ends through the folded end (*Fig. 1a*); draw the knot up **tightly** (*Fig. 1b*). Repeat along cast on and bind off edges for a total of 11 fringes on each end.

Slip bead on every other fringe and tie an overhand knot to secure bead.
Lay Scarf flat on a hard surface and trim the fringe.

Fig. 1a

Fig. 1b

OPTION

1

For the real trendsetter, only a **one-of-a-kind** boa scarf will do! Knitted from super bulky weight yarn, it's an accessory you can wear with the assurance that you're setting the **fashion curve**.

Lighten up on your yarn weight while changing your color palette. It's as **simple** as using a variegated bulky weight yarn. Whatever yarn you choose, the fast **fringing** technique makes your boa finish in a flash.

OPTION 2

Option 1

Adrienne Vittadini® Nadia
Super Bulky Weight Yarn
[1³/₄ ounces, 71 yards (50 grams, 65 meters)
per skein]: #800 (Black & White) - 1 skein

Straight knitting needles, size 11 (8 mm) **or**
size needed for gauge
Stitch holder

GAUGE: In pattern, 12 sts = 4" (10 cm)

WILD AT HEART ▰▰▱▱ EASY

Option 2

Lion Brand® Homespun®
Bulky Weight Yarn
[6 ounces, 185 yards (170 grams, 167 meters)
per skein]: #345 Corinthian - 1 skein

Straight knitting needles, size 11 (8 mm) **or**
size needed for gauge
Stitch holder

GAUGE: In pattern, 12 sts = 4" (10 cm)

STITCH GUIDE

KNIT ANCHOR STITCH
Knit into the front and the back loop of the next st *(Figs. 2a & b, page 47).* Pass the second st on right needle over the first st.

PURL ANCHOR STITCH
Purl into the front and the back loop of the next st *(Fig. 3, page 47).* Pass the second st on right needle over the first st.

Boa

Cast on 15 sts.

Row 1 (Right side)**:** K5, work knit Anchor st, K3, work knit Anchor st, K5.

Row 2: P5, work purl Anchor st, P3, work purl Anchor st, P5.

Repeat Rows 1 and 2 for pattern until Boa measures approximately 36" (91.5 cm) from cast on edge **or** until desired length, ending by working Row 2. (Boa will get longer after fringe is formed.)

Last Row: K5 and place sts just worked on st holder, bind off next 4 sts, cut yarn and pull end through loop, leaving last 5 sts unworked.

FRINGE

Working on one side at a time, unravel the 5 edge sts on every row, one row at a time, tying an overhand knot at base of each loop, close to piece. Cut loops.
If "frizzy" fringe is desired, carefully use a comb to brush fringe and create "frizzy" edges.

EXOTIC OPTION 1

Traditional yarns are spun to make them **fluffy**. But ribbon yarn is woven flat. Take your knitting into a **surprising** new world of dimension — create a fluttery boa of looped ribbon yarn. **Truly exotic!**

Content, width, weave — the structure of ribbon yarn gives you lots of choices — and it lets you decide how much **"body"** your boa will have. For relaxed loops, choose a soft ribbon yarn. For loops that retain their shape, simply use a firm ribbon yarn. The **options** are always yours.

EXOTIC

② OPTION

EXOTIC

 EASY

Trendsetter Yarns® Checkmate   SUPER BULKY **6**
Super Bulky Weight Ribbon Yarn
[1³/₄ ounces, 70 yards (50 grams, 64 meters)
per ball]: #902 (Black) - 2 balls

Straight knitting needles, size 17 (12.75 mm) **or**
size needed for gauge
Stitch holder

GAUGE: In pattern, 10 sts = 3" (7.5 cm)

Option 2

Caron® Pizazz   SUPER BULKY **6**
Super Bulky Weight Ribbon Yarn
[1³/₄ ounces, 28 yards (50 grams, 26 meters)
per ball]: #0001 Birthday - 5 balls

Straight knitting needles, size 17 (12.75 mm) **or**
size needed for gauge
Stitch holder

GAUGE: In pattern, 10 sts = 3" (7.5 cm)

36

STITCH GUIDE
ANCHOR STITCH
Knit into the front and back loop of the next st (*Figs. 2a & b, page 47*). Pass the second st on right needle over the first st.

Boa

Cast on 10 sts.

Row 1: K2, work Anchor st, K4, work Anchor st, K2.

Repeat Row 1 for pattern until Boa measures approximately 63" (160 cm) from cast on edge. (Boa will get longer after fringe is formed.)

Last Row: K2 and place sts just worked on st holder, bind off next 5 sts, cut yarn and pull end through loop, leaving last 2 sts unworked.

FRINGE
Working on one side at a time, unravel the 2 edge sts on every row.

Add fringe down center of Boa as follows: Working off the ball of ribbon yarn, thread yarn needle with end. Insert needle from front to back through center st on bound off edge. Weave ribbon yarn along center of Boa, going under one ridge and over one ridge and being careful not to catch side loops; secure end of ribbon yarn in center st on cast on edge.
Beginning at cast on edge, pull first strand on front to form a loop 1" (2.5 cm) longer than the side loops; tie loop in an overhand knot. Continue in same manner for each strand on front, pulling ribbon yarn from ball as needed; secure end.

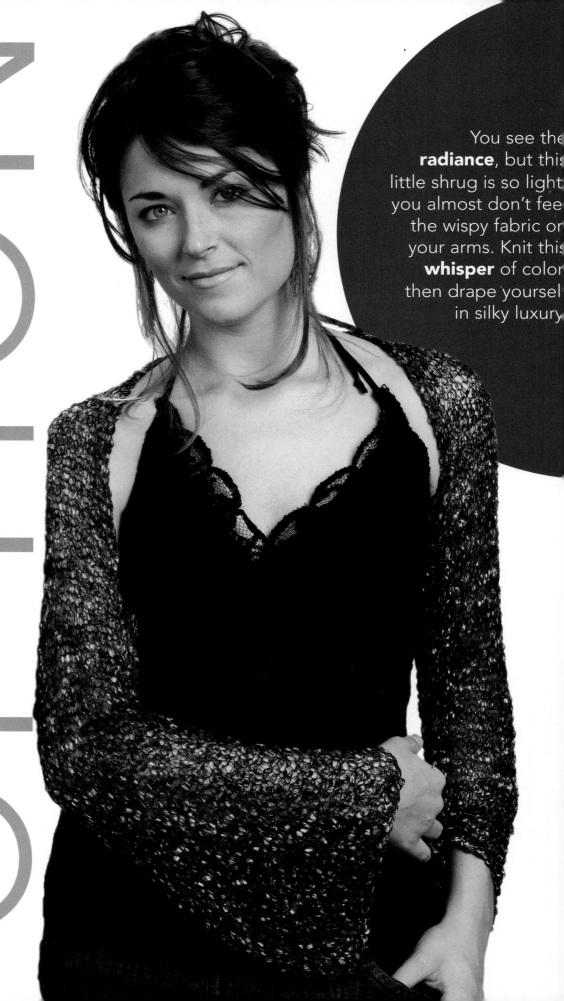

OPTION

1

You see the **radiance**, but this little shrug is so light you almost don't feel the wispy fabric on your arms. Knit this **whisper** of color then drape yourself in silky luxury.

Vibrant hues are the only thing keeping this **ethereal** accessory from floating away. And since wearing this shrug is quite a bit like wrapping yourself in a smile, be sure to choose lightweight ribbon yarn in colors that make you **happy**.

OPTION 2

Option 1

Caron® Fabulous

Light Weight Yarn
[1³/₄ ounces, 160 yards (50 grams, 146 meters) per ball]: #0015 Mother Earth - 2{3-3} balls

Circular knitting needle, size 11 (8 mm) **or** size needed for gauge
Yarn needle

GAUGE: In Stockinette Stitch, 16 sts = 4" (10 cm)

WEAR A WHISPER ◖□□□ BEGINNER

Option 2

FFF® Karnack

Light Weight Yarn
[1 ounce, 103 yards (25 grams, 94 meters) per ball]: #3008 Pink Lime - 4{5-6} balls

Circular knitting needle, size 11 (8 mm) **or** size needed for gauge
Yarn needle

GAUGE: In Stockinette Stitch, 16 sts = 4" (10 cm)

Size	Finished Length	
Small	52"	(132 cm)
Medium	56"	(142 cm)
Large	60"	(152.5 cm)

Note: Instructions are written for size Small with sizes Medium and Large in braces { }. Instructions will be easier to read if you circle all the numbers pertaining to your size. If only one number is given, it applies to all sizes.

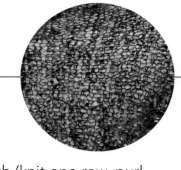

Shrug

Cast on 52{58-64} sts.

Work in Stockinette Stitch (knit one row, purl one row) until Shrug measures approximately 52{56-60}"/132{142-152.5} cm from cast on edge.

Bind off all sts as loose as the cast on edge.

With **right** side together, fold Shrug in half lengthwise; whipstitch each end of long edge forming sleeves *(Fig. 8, page 48)*, leaving the center 20{22-24}"/51{56-61} cm free.

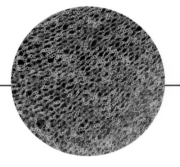

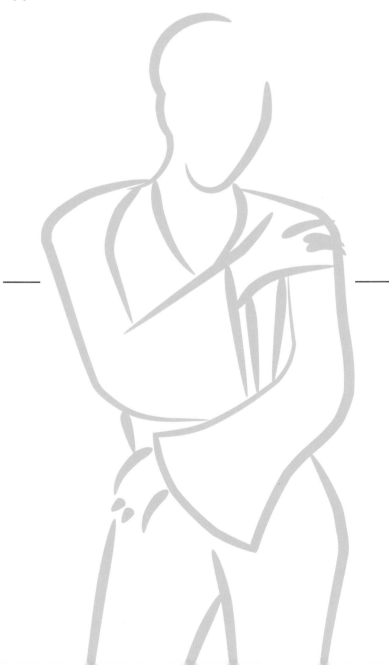

HEAVEN & EARTH

OPTION

1

How about something **fresh** for summer? A white shrug of cotton tape will transform your sleeveless tops while allowing you to enjoy every **cool breeze** that comes your way.

The same shrug becomes an **entirely different** accessory when you use a bulky weight yarn in earth tones. Pair this **earthy** version with your favorite spring and autumn tops.

Rowan International® Cotton Tape
Bulky Weight Yarn
[1.75 ounces, 71 yards (50 grams, 65 meters)
per skein]: #540 White - 5{6-6} skeins

Straight knitting needles, size 15 (10 mm) **or**
size needed for gauge
Yarn needle

GAUGE: In pattern, 12 sts = 4½" (11.5 cm)

HEAVEN & EARTH

 EASY

Bernat® Softee Chunky
Bulky Weight Yarn
[2.8 ounces, 134 yards (80 grams, 123 meters)
per skein]: #40012 Nature's Way - 3{4-4} skeins

Straight knitting needles, size 15 (10 mm) **or**
size needed for gauge
Yarn needle

GAUGE: In pattern, 12 sts = 4½" (11.5 cm)

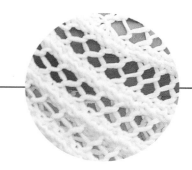

Size	Finished Length	
Small	52"	(132 cm)
Medium	55"	(139.5 cm)
Large	58"	(147.5 cm)

Note: Instructions are written for size Small with sizes Medium and Large in braces { }. Instructions will be easier to read if you circle all the numbers pertaining to your size. If only one number is given, it applies to all sizes.

Shrug

Cast on 40{44-48} sts.

Row 1: K3, P1, YO *(Fig. 4b, page 47)*, P2 tog *(Fig. 7, page 48)*, ★ K1, P1, YO, P2 tog; repeat from ★ across to last 2 sts, K2.

Repeat Row 1 for pattern, until Shrug measures approximately 52{55-58}"/132{139.5-147.5} cm from cast on edge.

Bind off all sts as loose as the cast on edge.

Fold Shrug in half lengthwise; whipstitch each end of long edge forming sleeves *(Fig. 8, page 48)*, leaving the center 20{22-24}"/51{56-61} cm free.

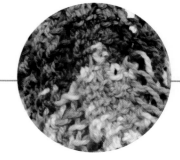

GENERAL

ABBREVIATIONS

cm	centimeters	SSK	slip, slip, knit
K	knit	st(s)	stitch(es)
mm	millimeters	tog	together
P	purl	YO	yarn over

★ — work instructions following ★ as many **more** times as indicated in addition to the first time.

( ) or [ ] — work enclosed instructions **as many** times as specified by the number immediately following **or** contains explanatory remarks.

colon (:) — the number(s) given after a colon at the end of a row or round denote(s) the number of stitches or spaces you should have on that row or round.

GAUGE

Exact gauge is **essential** for proper size. Before beginning your project, make a sample swatch in the yarn and needle specified. After completing the swatch, measure it, counting your stitches and rows carefully. If your swatch is larger or smaller than specified, **make another, changing needle size to get the correct gauge.** Keep trying until you find the size needles that will give you the specified gauge.

KNITTING NEEDLES		
UNITED STATES	**ENGLISH U.K.**	**METRIC (mm)**
0	13	2
1	12	2.25
2	11	2.75
3	10	3.25
4	9	3.5
5	8	3.75
6	7	4
7	6	4.5
8	5	5
9	4	5.5
10	3	6
10½	2	6.5
11	1	8
13	00	9
15	000	10
17	---	12.75
19	---	15

KNIT TERMINOLOGY	
UNITED STATES	**INTERNATIONAL**
gauge =	tension
bind off =	cast off
yarn over (YO) =	yarn forward (yfwd) **or**
	yarn around needle (yrn)

Yarn Weight Symbol & Names	SUPER FINE 1	FINE 2	LIGHT 3	MEDIUM 4	BULKY 5	SUPER BULKY 6
Type of Yarns in Category	Sock, Fingering Baby	Sport, Baby	DK, Light Worsted	Worsted, Afghan, Aran	Chunky, Craft, Rug	Bulky, Roving
Knit Gauge Ranges in Stockinette St to 4" (10 cm)	27-32 sts	23-26 sts	21-24 sts	16-20 sts	12-15 sts	6-11 sts
Advised Needle Size Range	1-3	3-5	5-7	7-9	9-11	11 and larger

◼◻◻◻ BEGINNER	Projects for first-time knitters using basic knit and purl stitches. Minimal shaping.
◼◼◻◻ EASY	Projects using basic stitches, repetitive stitch patterns, simple color changes, and simple shaping and finishing.
◼◼◼◻ INTERMEDIATE	Projects with a variety of stitches, such as basic cables and lace, simple intarsia, double-pointed needles and knitting in the round needle techniques, mid-level shaping and finishing.
◼◼◼◼ EXPERIENCED	Projects using advanced techniques and stitches, such as short rows, fair isle, more intricate intarsia, cables, lace patterns, and numerous color changes.

INSTRUCTIONS

HINTS

Good finishing techniques make a big difference in the quality of the piece. Do not tie knots. Always start a new ball at the beginning of a row, leaving ends long enough to weave in later. Thread a yarn needle with the yarn end. With **wrong** side facing, weave the needle through several inches, then reverse the direction and weave it back through several inches. When ends are secure, clip them off close to work.

KNIT INCREASE

Knit the next stitch but do **not** slip the old stitch off the left needle *(Fig. 2a)*. Insert the right needle into the **back** loop of the **same** stitch and knit it *(Fig. 2b)*, then slip the old stitch off the left needle.

Fig. 2a

Fig. 2b

PURL INCREASE

Purl the next stitch but do **not** slip the old stitch off the left needle. Insert the right needle into the **back** loop of the **same** stitch from **back** to **front** *(Fig. 3)* and purl it. Slip the old stitch off the left needle.

Fig. 3

YARN OVERS *(abbreviated YO)*

After a knit stitch, before a knit stitch
Bring the yarn forward **between** the needles, then back **over** the top of the right hand needle, so that it is now in position to knit the next stitch *(Fig. 4a)*.

Fig. 4a

After a purl stitch, before a purl stitch
Take yarn **over** the right hand needle to the back, then forward **under** it, so that it is now in position to purl the next stitch *(Fig. 4b)*.

Fig. 4b

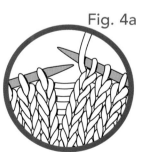

KNIT 2 TOGETHER
(abbreviated K2 tog)

Insert the right needle into the **front** of the first two stitches on the left needle as if to **knit** *(Fig. 5)*, then **knit** them together as if they were one stitch.

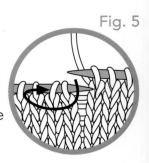
Fig. 5

SLIP, SLIP, KNIT
(abbreviated SSK)

With yarn in back of work, separately slip two stitches as if to **knit** *(Fig. 6a)*. Insert the **left** needle into the **front** of both slipped stitches *(Fig. 6b)* and knit them together as if they were one stitch *(Fig. 6c)*.

Fig. 6a

Fig. 6b

Fig. 6c

PURL 2 TOGETHER
(abbreviated P2 tog)

Insert the right needle into the **front** of the first two stitches on the left needle as if to **purl** *(Fig. 7)*, then **purl** them together as if they were one stitch.

Fig. 7

WHIPSTITCH

With **right** sides together, sew through both pieces once to secure the beginning of the seam, leaving an ample yarn end to weave in later. Insert the needle from front to back through one strand on each piece *(Fig. 8)*. Bring the needle around and insert it from front to back through the next strand on both pieces. Repeat along the edge, being careful to match rows.

Fig. 8